Wade's World

TRIUMPH
BOOKS

Published by Triumph Books, Chicago.

Text by David Hyde

Photography by Marc Serota except were noted below.

AP/Wide World Photos on pages: 5, 22-27, 31, 33-43, 45, 75, 81, 82, 97, 101, 102.

Content packaged by Mojo Media, Inc.
Editor: Joe Funk
Creative Director: Jason Hinman

This book is available in quantity at special discounts for your group or organization.
For further information, contact:

Triumph Books
542 South Dearborn Street
Suite 750
Chicago, IL 60605

Chicago, Illinois 60605
Phone: (312) 939-3330
Fax: (312) 663-3557

Printed in the United States of America

Contents

Look At Him Now

It's official: a new superstar has arrived

For two years, his agent had been telling him this sweet spot would come. And when it did—starting from the moment he flung a celebratory basketball toward the sky in Dallas— Dwyane Wade's summer of love began. He joked on *Jimmy Kimmel Live!* He laughed on MTV.

There were movie scripts coming in, endorsement deals to weigh, a Disney World parade to lead, a *Time* magazine story to give. There was a seat beside David Letterman, who told him, "You know who was on here last week was Mark Cuban, who owns the Dallas Mav..."

Dwyane Wade

"Who? Who's that?" Wade interrupted.

Letterman laughed. "What do you say to a guy like that who's making all kind of noise about the referees were controlling the outcome of the games?"

Wade turned a street-cold stare on Letterman. Said nothing. Shook his head back and forth slowly. One second passed. Two seconds. Then, with comedic timing and a runway smile, Wade allowed everyone in on the joke.

"Don't even acknowledge him," Wade said.

The audience applauded. Letterman delivered his trademark staccato laugh.

By then, Wade was on the Wheaties box and the *Sports Illustrated* cover. His No. 3 jersey was No. 1 in sales among NBA players. His $90 signature Converse shoe, released in eight color schemes, was a top seller among basketball sneakers. At the NBA draft, the golden measuring stick, as TV analysts and basketball pundits said, was whether there was a, "next Dwyane Wade."

So he was popping up everywhere that summer, literally, conversationally and often physically. He woke up early for Regis and Kelly in New York, did the Best Damn Sports Show poolside in Las Vegas and joked with actor Ashley Judd at the ESPY Awards in Los Angeles about beating her Kentucky team a few years earlier in the NCAA Tournament.

He also looked down at the ESPY program in his hand later that night when female musical stars walked past him. Only he didn't have a program in his hand. His wife noticed.

"You can look," said his wife, Siohvaughn.

Even stars have stars they admire. Wade gave a peek, smiling as he did.

Two years earlier, after first bursting on the national scene in his rookie playoffs, Wade's agent, Henry Thomas, had called around to companies about possible endorsement deals. Some didn't return the call. Some did with a, "cordial, 'We'll watch him, and see what he becomes,'" Thomas remembered.

Thomas saw what was coming on the horizon. He

Dwyane and his wife, Siohvaughn, started dating in high school, got married in college, and have shared in Dwyane's remarkable rise to super stardom.

cautioned Wade that his star would rise and he should prepare himself accordingly. That way, the attention wouldn't emotionally swamp him in the manner it did other athletes. During Wade's second season the attention began, but now in the days after the Heat's championship season and Wade's breakthrough playoffs, it was something new every day. Something big.

"We call it our 'Bless Stress,'" Siohvaughn said.

There were too many companies calling him to count and so many deals that could be made. That wasn't even factoring in the biggest deal of them all—the three-year, $60-million deal he signed with the Heat a month after hoisting the Most Valuable Players trophy of the NBA Finals.

"I've been here and there and everywhere," he said

Wade's World

Dwyane welcomed Shaquille O'Neal to the Heat with open arms when Shaq arrived before the 2004-2005 season.

Dwyane Wade

Dwyane Wade

Perhaps taking the tradition of dressing in white for Heat home games a little too far, Miami fans are rabid supporters of Wade and the Heat.

at that news conference. "And everywhere I go all we talk about is the championship. Hopefully, people will never get tired of it, because I don't. It's a great, great accomplishment."

One thing he wouldn't do this summer: A movie. It wasn't because he didn't want to do one. It certainly wasn't for lack of desire on Hollywood's part as scripts were pouring in—suspense, adventure, you name it, he could play the part.

Wade had no time to shoot a movie this summer. As if jet-setting around the country for premiere shows wasn't enough, Team USA beckoned. The World Championships took up half of July and all of August. Unlike at the 2004 Athens Olympics, when Wade slid onto the roster because bigger stars had

backed out, no one wondered about his role on the American team anymore.

In some respects, the last thing he wanted after a long, physically and emotionally draining season was to play basketball for six more weeks. But as soon as he stepped on the floor at the practice site in Las Vegas and saw the all-star talent around him, that thought vanished. His competitive spirit kicked in. So did his team-first desire to win, so much so that as the games began he went to coach Mike Krzyzewski and asked something completely in-character but out of the realm of most players' thinking: "Can I come off the bench?"

He had started four games to that point with Team USA. He was averaging 21.4 points. But Wade saw coming off the bench as a way to give the Americans a ferocious one-two punch of LeBron James and Carmelo Anthony among the starters and himself lifting the second unit.

"Coming off the bench gives this team another

Wade's World

Dwyane Wade has stolen some of the spotlight away from fellow 2004 NBA rookie classmate, and ultra-hyped, LeBron James where it matters most: On the court.

Dwyane Wade

Wade's MVP trophy sits in his locker with empty champagne bottles after a Game 6 victory over the Dallas Mavericks for the 2006 NBA Championship.

dimension and I love it," Wade said.

A superstar benching himself and suppressing his ego might not be the way the sporting world usually works these days. But that's the player the Heat had come to know by then. He was being called the anti-Kobe for playing the game at dizzying heights but thinking first of winning. And while a title went to his ring finger and brought him new riches, it didn't go to his head.

"It's a short summer, but a pretty productive summer," he said. "Most of what's happening is stuff I didn't even dream about. I dreamed of playing basketball. Talk shows, magazine covers, movies—I didn't even know to think of that."

As he talked, he was seated in a room under American Airlines Arena. It was the same room he had been introduced to South

Florida three years prior, when the Heat drafted him. The Heat was in transition at the time of his arrival: Alonzo Mourning was suffering from a kidney illness; a roll of the dice was made to bring free agent Lamar Odom to the team; and Pat Riley would turn over the coaching reins to unheralded Stan Van Gundy the week before the season began.

No one knew much about the Wade who arrived in that room three years ago. But he wasn't that different from the one who stood there after winning the title three years later. Everything around him has changed. But his core has stayed the same, from the kid in Chicago to the rising surprise at Marquette to the newest face of the NBA after a championship season.

"I remember sitting here in this room in a white suit after being drafted, just being a kid, just being excited, just happy to be in the NBA," he said. "Now here I am, having a world championship, Finals MVP. It's all happened so fast. It can be overwhelming. But I'm taking it in stride every step of the way that I'm the one God's chosen." ●

Wade's World

Keepin' It Real

Wade's Chicago roots run strong and deep

There wasn't a phone, a new car or any loose money lying around the small, one-story home on Claire Street. There was a basketball hoop out back, though, as well as a light behind the home that allowed everyone playing to hold onto the day a little longer, for just a few more points. That's all they ever wanted anyhow.

Typically on the court there was Dwyane Wade Sr., his two step-sons and the youngest and smallest of them all, the father's namesake, Dwyane Jr. They'd get up to play early in the morning. They'd play again late in the afternoon and into the night.

Dwyane Wade

These often were ordinary games in one sense: Two-on-two. Games to 11. Baskets count as one. Make it, take it. You had to win by two.

In another way, these games weren't so ordinary. They were father-and-son often without the typical father-son camaraderie. The kids weren't given anything on the court in the way they wouldn't be given anything of it. You wanted it? Come and earn it, Dwyane Sr. said.

"He'd have us back there, bleeding," the younger Dwyane says, smiling as he looks back.

There was some home-court advantage involved for the father. He would run the kids into gates. He would block the ball near a pit bull tied in the corner, and the kids think twice before retrieving it. Mostly, though, if you tried to drive the lane on him you could find yourself planted in the ground.

This is where Wade learned how to drive inside and, when knocked down, as he often was by his father, he learned how to fall in a way to protect his body. This is where, if he began playing wrong, his father would demand he practice the same skill over and over.

This, too, is where he learned to walk like his Chicago hero, Michael Jordan, right down to chewing the gum the same way.

He hadn't moved into the home until he was eight. His sister, Tragil, then 13, took him on a bus ride then from the south side of Chicago to the suburb of Robbins, which the locals always call "Mudville." Young Dwyane thought it was a quick trip on an ordinary day to see his father, who was divorced from his mother. The rest of the family didn't tell him the move was permanent to keep him from the reach of gangs. They talked about it amongst themselves and made the decision.

So it was here where Wade attended the Blood, Water and Spirit Ministry, a church that remains the focus of his tithing a Biblical 10 percent of his salary.

It was here at the Robbins Community Center where Wade honed his young game. Three of the

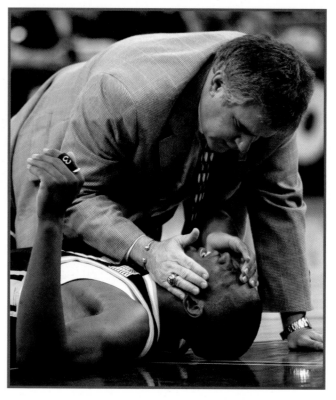

Marquette trainer Steve Condon checks out Wade after he got hit in the eye.

four rims are bent today, the nets tattered.

Here, too, his future wife, Siohvaughn, lived. A year older, she became part of a group that befriended Wade after he moved to Robbins and called him "Puff," for his sleepy-eyed look. She became Wade's girlfriend when he was a high-school junior and she a senior. She took it upon herself after noticing he had grown four inches over that summer, that he wasn't little Dwyane anymore.

She became his fiancée during his freshman year at Marquette after he proposed over a steak and potato dinner in her home at Christmas break. He had bought the ring at Montgomery Ward. He got on his knee to propose.

In the summer after that freshman year, while Wade was in Italy playing with a touring U.S. team, he got a phone call from Siohvaughn. She was preg-

Wade shares a laugh with Carmelo Anthony, another one of the players selected before Wade in the 2004 NBA Draft.

USA Basketball team members Dwyane Wade and LeBron James relax after a workout in Seoul, South Korea where Team USA played exhibition games prior to the World Championships in late summer, 2006.

Dwyane Wade

nant with their son, Zaire. He rented a tuxedo and she wore her dress from their H.L. Richards High School prom, and they got married.

Today at that high school, Wade's basketball shoes from the 2004 Olympics sit in a trophy case. The memories of him run deeper, though. Ask the teachers who remember him as honor-roll student at Richards, answering them with respective tones of, "Yes, ma'am," and "No, sir."

Ask his math teacher, Alyisa Porrello. She taught Wade for four years. A few years after he had graduated she received a letter from him. He wrote how much he enjoyed her class and thanked her for all her help. At the top of the letter he had written: "The NBA Awaits."

This place meant something to him that way. Even after he was making NBA millions, after he played a

Wade, representing Team USA, offers a hand salute as he and other members of the squad arrive at Yongsan Army base gymnasium for a practice session.

bad Game 1 against Detroit in the 2005 Eastern Conference finals, he called his high school coach, Tom Fitzgerald.

Fitzgerald was on the 17th tee at River Oaks Golf Club in Chicago, but Wade just wanted some pick-me-up perspective. Fitzgerald reminded Wade of his awful game his senior year against Thornton High, maybe the worst of his high school days. The next night game, Fitzgerald said, was one of his best. Wade took toe advice to heart and came back to score 40 points in Game 2 against Detroit.

At Richards, though, Wade didn't appear to be pre-destined for stardom early on. He couldn't

Wade listens to the national anthem
before Game 3 of the NBA Finals.

dunk until his sophomore year. He didn't make the varsity team until he was a junior. Once on the team, however, he quickly became a rare commodity on the basketball court—in his senior year he scored 90 points in the same day in two tournament games.

Still, as a late-bloomer, he was lost amid the entitled world of prep basketball. When Nike picked 11 Chicago-area kids to come to its camp after his junior season, he wasn't one on the list. He didn't get to any prestigious all-star camps at all. That cut down his visibility with college recruiters. It hurt even more when his college-entrance exam scores didn't qualify him for freshman eligibility.

Only three schools seriously recruited him: Marquette, DePaul and Illinois State. He sat down with Siohvaughn's mother and Fitzgerald and discussed the options. This would be how he would make the big decisions in his life, leaning on those closest to him and going over each possibility. In the end, he chose Marquette. It had been the first to contact him, and the first to visit him. He trusted Marquette's coach, Tom Crean.

He never left Robbins behind. Each summer, he has a basketball clinic in his old neighborhood, showing youth who they can become and reminding himself who he is. He remembers hearing about such clinics when he was a kid. A big-name celebrity would come back to his hometown. A playground would be chosen. Kids would pack the place. The only problem was no one ever came back to Robbins. Wade always looked at those other towns and thought they were the lucky ones. Now he hopes local kids will think the same when they attend his camp.

Of course, every day in Robbins has another reminder of their homegrown superstar. On the corner of Pulaski Road and Midlothian Turnpike, a sign sits outside where Fitzgerald and Tragil teach at Aspen High School. It's a small sign, simple, unpretentious and friendly just like the person it hails. It reads:

"Have a Nice Summer. Congrats Dwyane Wade of Robbins and Miami Heat." ●

A Bolt From the Blue

Wade emerges as a
star at Marquette

Pat Riley fell in basketball love with Dwyane Wade on a Stairmaster. That wasn't so unusual. The Heat coach had fallen in love with players everywhere across a life in the game. He fell in love with Magic Johnson from behind a radio microphone. He fell in love with Alonzo Mourning watching him run sprints.

So it was that Riley sweated on a Stairmaster in a Milwaukee hotel in March of 2003, watching the televised NCAA Tournament game between his alma mater, Kentucky, and Marquette. Kentucky was the top seed in its tournament region. It had won 26 straight games. It had rich history and blue chip pedigree, of which Riley was a part.

Marquette had Wade.

In one telling first-half stretch, Wade sparked a Marquette run with seven points, two assists and a soaring block of a shot of Kentucky's 6-9 Marquis Estill.

"You better draft him," another exerciser told Riley.

"Ain't no way a Kentucky guy can draft him," Riley exclaimed.

Wade, a junior, was a first-team All-American by then. He was one of five finalists for the John Wooden Award as the best collegiate player. He had scored 20 points in the second half against Pittsburgh two days earlier to advance to the Kentucky game and bring a national spotlight fully on his small school.

Now, against Kentucky, he was ending any thought he would return for his senior season. He had wondered about the NBA for weeks, until this day when he sunk Kentucky with 29 points, 11 rebounds and 11 assists. It sent Marquette to the Final Four. It was just the fourth triple-double in NCAA Tournament history. It made Kansas coach Roy Williams say, "I'm not trying to say this because you shouldn't compare anybody to Michael Jordan, but it was scary all the things he could do. I looked a couple times to make sure it was still No. 3 (Wade's jersey number) I was watching on tape and not No. 23."

That run also capped Wade's three-year college evolution from unknown talent to certain lottery NBA pick. He had sat out his freshman year at Marquette, to improve his academics. Meanwhile, Marquette coach Tom Crean didn't want Wade to drift through a season without games and set up a plan to assure it.

Wade was put on a weightlifting program for the first time in his life and added muscled weight to his frame. In practice, he regularly was matched up against Brian Wardle, a tough senior who either

would demand Wade compete or pound him into submission. Wardle remembers the freshman Wade as a raw player with the requisite set of physical talent and basketball IQ for stardom. As that season wore on, "It got harder and harder for me to go against him," Wardle said.

Dwyane Wade

Wade was also given the assignment of mimicking the opponent's top player in practice. Some games that player would be a guard, other games a forward. That demanded Wade become more versatile and added to his tool set of skills. Eventually, he would play shooting guard, small forward and even occasionally power forward in college.

Finally that freshman season, Crean demanded Wade stand with the coaches at halftime and face the team as it was addressed. Occasionally, Crean would put his freshman on the spot, as one game when he asked Wade on a scale of 1 to 10 how a certain player was doing.

"A two," Wade answered.

Somehow, even as a non-playing freshman, he had the ability to be honest without giving a trace of meanness. And when he began playing for the first time as sophomore season there was no doubt he had the game to back up his words. He was named honorable mention All-American that year. It all set up a senior year in which he averaged 21.5 points, 6.3 rebounds and 4.4 assists in leading the Golden Eagles on its NCAA Tournament run.

He wasn't just another pretty scorer, though. He was the Conference USA Defensive Player of the Year as a senior, clamping down on the opponents' top scorer and averaging 12 deflections a game. His high was 22 deflections in a game his final season.

So he had an impressive collegiate portfolio as he considered whether to leave for the NBA after his junior season. His decision wasn't much of one after NBA people said how high he could be drafted. He had a family with his wife and 1-year-old son. He also had climbed the college mountain, as his achievements showed.

"I can further my education or I can live my dream out," Wade said in announcing his decision to turn pro.

Two weeks before the draft, the Heat flew Wade to Miami for a workout. The franchise was in dreadful shape. It was coming off 36- and 25-win seasons as it recovered from the loss of Alonzo Mourning to kidney disease. It averaged just 85.6 point the previous season, second worst in the NBA. And it had no proven guards.

It's a good thing first impressions weren't lasting. Wade's workout couldn't have gone much worse. He missed shots. He didn't move well with the ball. He seemed to grow tense. Nothing seemed to go right.

As they talked afterward, Riley and general manager Randy Pfund downplayed the workout's results. They instead liked how mature Wade seemed in talking to them, how ready his game looked on tape for the NBA. Pfund remembered one game in which Wade didn't shoot particularly well (9 of 23) but ended with a smorgasbord of 24 points, eight rebounds, seven assists and two steals.

"That was a typical Dwyane Wade game," Pfund said. "He didn't start out fast and, as the game went on, you kind of said, 'When's Dwyane gonna get going here?' Then he had a great ball game."

Riley, in particular, studied how he performed at the end of games.

"That's the true measure of a player," Riley said. "How he finished is what really sets him apart. He wanted the ball. He wanted to decide games. That's the kind of quality you looked for and it came naturally to him."

Still, Riley hoped the Heat didn't end up with Wade on draft night. It's like he was the door prize. In a sport where size is most coveted, the Heat had hoped the 6-10 Chris Bosh would slip past Toronto and into their hands. That Toronto had the fourth pick, and the Heat the fifth, was a circumstance traced to the season finale between the two teams. The loser received the sweeter draft spot. Riley remembered playing reserves for season-high minutes that night and still winning the game but losing the real reward.

Toronto took Bosh.

The Heat got Wade.

Riley, thinking how it fell together, later said, "The basketball gods gave us one." ●

Rookie Redemption

A promising
first year sets the
stage for a new
American idol

Here's an idea you don't hear enough in professional sports: Dwyane Wade became so good during his rookie season by admitting he wasn't good enough. He could only dribble the basketball hard with his left hand once or twice before losing control. His mid-range jump shot was shaky. He had little balance when he shot the ball.

"I'm just blending in," he said after his first training camp.

"I've got to do more," he said in December.

Wade announces he is going pro as his college coach, Tom Crean, looks on.

"Some nights when I score 20-something points, I walk away and say I didn't play very well," he said in April.

Wade meant it, too. He acted on it. He was there after practice, every day, taking an extra hundred shots, working on details like dribbling and footwork. He kept adding small pieces to his game that, linked together over time, would complete the bigger, lethal picture. The NBA is full of players who see only strengths. But all his basketball life Wade had been forced to face shortcomings so that, as he moved forward, he could look back to understand how these disadvantages became his biggest advantages:

• He didn't play varsity until a junior in high school.

• He couldn't get an invitation to the prestigious sneaker camps for the best prep players.

• He was only recruited by three colleges.

• He was considered an NBA draft afterthought in the year of LeBron James and Carmelo Anthony.

That helps explain why complementing Wade's great physical skills by the time he reached the NBA was an overachievers' work ethic. All his life he had to work harder to earn his place. He didn't feel entitled to have a NBA job. He smiled when he saw fans wearing his jersey in the same manner he once wore the jerseys of Michael Jordan and Kevin Garnett.

Wade wasn't just open to constructive coaching at the NBA level. He thirsted for it. That might not have been the standard way for a rookie coming into his first money. But it's the only way Wade knew.

"He worked on something you don't hear much at this level–fundamentals," Heat coach Stan Van Gundy said after Wade's rookie year. "A lot of guys who have had the kind of year Dwyane has had would look at you weird if you said they needed to work on jumping straight up and down to improve your jump shot.

'Come on, I'm a superstar.' "

"But right now, that's what he's working on. Jumping up and down. Balance. Fundamentals. That's why he's going to be so great."

It didn't matter to Wade that his rookie season was a toasted success. After missing 20 early games with an ankle injury, his talent became obvious. He averaged 16.2 points on 47 percent shooting. He was the first rookie in four years to receive Player of the Week honors. He made the All-Rookie team. He even led a Heat team that weathered Pat Riley's coaching resignation and began the year 0-7, to the second round of the playoffs.

Through all that, Wade knew what had to be done. His moment of moments that season confirmed just where this work could take him. In Game 1 of the opening playoff series, he drove by New Orleans guard Baron Davis, hung in the air for an extended second and made the winning shot with 1.3 seconds left.

Dwyane Wade

For fans, it was a statement of immediate impact and coming greatness. Among the inner Heat circle, however, the play was seen as a culmination of months of hard work by Wade.

"When we first got him, that first summer, he did all his work from half-court to the free-throw line," Riley said. "Beating guys off the dribble. How far do you go? What decisions to make? When he beat Baron Davis on that drive in the playoffs, he had done that drill 1,000 times or more with (Heat assistant) Eric Spoelstra," Riley said.

Wade built on that moment, too. He had double figures in points (12) and rebounds (11) in Game 4 of that New Orleans series. In Game 6, he hit the deciding 3-point shot. At the opener of the next series against Indiana, Siohvaughn made a sign that she held up at Thursday's game.

"Last Rookie Standing," it read.

There was no LeBron, no Carmelo, no Chris Bosh playing by then. Wade, for once, had the young-gun stage to his own. Later that summer, the Athens Olympics would confirm Wade's standing. Though he felt handcuffed by coach Larry Brown's style, Wade fit into the team concept and contributed to the bronze-medal-winning U.S. Team while his fellow rookies groused and sat on the bench.

Watching Wade grow that first season was like seeing time-elapsed film of a kid growing up. As Riley reflected on who Wade was and how far he had come as a rookie season, he said something he couldn't have at the draft.

"He's on the brink of true greatness," Riley said. "I see it every night. He's forever attacking, probing, doing things, taking risks and creating incredible situations. I've not seen that since Michael Jordan."

There it was. That comparison to his boyhood idol, the one Wade would forever and humbly back away from. Riley didn't, though.

"I remember Jordan as a rookie," Riley said. "His first couple of years, even though there wasn't a full awareness, there was this incredible talent going in different directions. You saw once he became mature and savvy and professional, it was going to be directed in the right way. It took Michael seven or eight years to become that champion. I just see Dwyane with many of the same things. And, like Michael, he's ultra-competitive. That makes the talent burgeon."

Meanwhile, another basketball surprise was coming that summer to accelerate Wade's progress even more. ●

Wade's World

Always a solid teammate, Wade chest-thumps with Antoine Walker after a key play.

Superheroes Unite!

Shaq comes to town to form a dynamic duo

The phone call came as Dwyane Wade drove to the ESPY Awards in Los Angeles.

"I'm going to cross-over (dribble) on you the first day of practice," Shaquille O'Neal said by way of introduction.

And so right there, in the opening seconds following a climactic trade, O'Neal and Wade had something bitterly missing from O'Neal's relationship with Lakers' teammate Kobe Bryant. Laughter. And respect. And as the conversation turned serious, O'Neal and Wade underlined the importance of making their relationship work because, as they knew, how they went so went the team.

O'Neal, at 32, had lobbied for the Heat to trade anyone but Wade to Los Angeles. He knew the value of a star outside presence to counter his inside game. In fact, when Pat Riley called to announce the trade was completed, O'Neal's first words were, "Who'd you have to give up?"

Publicly then, O'Neal was gracious toward his new partner ("I came to Miami because of Dwyane Wade") and even humble ("The mistakes I made with Penny Hardaway and Kobe Bryant I won't make with Dwyane Wade").

Publicly, too, Wade immediately gave two thumbs up to the trade, asking, "How couldn't you want Shaq on your team? This gives us a chance for a title."

Privately, however, there lingered a nagging issue with Wade. He knew O'Neal was a force of nature. He knew of the titles he won and the chance he brought to win more. But it's what Wade didn't know that gave him pause. Namely, how would Wade play in the upcoming season without teammates that had a good chemistry developing the season before?

This was his first, hardened look at the business side of sport. He hadn't just won with Lamar Odom, Brian Grant and Caron Butler, who now were Lakers. Butler had become his best friend on the team. The day of the trade, Butler later said, Wade, "called me 10 times, saying, 'This is crazy.' "

Shaq quickly became the dominant inside force the Heat had hoped for when they maneuvered to get him from the Lakers in one of the biggest trades in NBA history.

What's more, Wade heard whispers how he would be pushed to the background by O'Neal's spotlight. It's true, O'Neal's grand entrance to Miami showed how much bigger than 7-foot-1 and 330 pounds he actually was. It was a presidential inauguration. Red carpet. Police escort. Cheering thousands. A banner hung from the arena saying, "Shaq in Black." And then came the man himself, driving up to the front of American Arilines Arena in an 18-wheeler that read "Diesel Power" on the side and "Man of Steel" on the cab, squirting fans with a water gun.

He came armed with a promise, too.

"I'm going to bring a championship to Miami," he shouted.

Yep, Shaq knew how to make an entrance. Wade could appreciate that. He just wondered how it would all fit together. This came at a time Wade was just making a breakthrough, too. His game had proved it could carry a team. Endorsers also were calling after his rookie playoff run. His name was rising. Would all that downshift with O'Neal on board?

His agent, Henry Thomas, prophetically told him the opposite. This trade was the best thing for him, Thomas said.

"You're going to be on the big stage, night in and night out," he said.

Wade received an off-court sampling of what his agent meant when a Miami car dealer approached O'Neal about endrosing them in return for an upper-end car. O'Neal said he had enough cars, but why not ask Wade? So there was Wade, driving a new, black Range Rover with tinted windows, a black-leather interior and "Flash" —the comic-book nickname given him by O'Neal— stenciled in the head rests.

In the coming year, other moments would follow to show his agent's read on Wade's risen star and Shaq's beneficial impact was right: A Times Square

billboard featuring Wade was erected by Converse; Sean John signed him to model its clothes; Gatorade put him in commercial with Derek Jeter and Peyton Manning; *Sports Illustrated For Kids* revealed every-thing from his favorite snack food (Honey Buns) to his favorite cartoon characters (Tom and Jerry); and he was selected to People magazine's "50 Most

Wade's World

Flash and Superman became fast friends, then got down to the business of bringing a title to Miami.

Dwyane Wade

Beautiful People" list.

"They must've picked from the neck down," teammate Damon Jones joked.

Wade said, dead-pan, "Where do you rank in the world?"

What he never lost amid all this was his drive for basketball. On the court that season, he kept putting moments in his scrapbook. He blocked Amare Stoudemare's shot in Phoenix, dribbled through traffic and made a 65-foot shot at the buzzer. He calmly let the clock tick down in Madison Square Garden before launching a game-winning shot and yelling at the crowd, "That's what I do!"

No regular-season stage was more anticipated than Shaq vs. Kobe I. Christmas Day. National television. But as O'Neal fouled out with the Heat down by two points, he turned to Wade and said, "Get this one for me." Wade took over down the stretch and finished with 29 points in the overtime win.

It was another day, and another singular move by Wade, that sent O'Neal into spasms of laughter in the locker room. At the end of a tight game in Utah, Wade began to drive on Raja Bell, who made a name for himself in the NBA by defending big scorers. Wade put the hard brakes on at the top of the key, though. Bell was so surprised that when he tried to shift his momentum his body kept going, stumbling, sending him to rest against the cushion at the backet's stanchion.

"He fell clear out of the picture," O'Neal said.

What Pat Riley hoped would happen when he traded for O'Neal happened naturally as the season progressed, too. Wade and O'Neal didn't simply become good teammates, complementing each other, Shaq's presence affording Wade more outside space and Wade's game lessening the demands on Shaq.

They also began to genuinely like each other. Part of it was each was bent on winning a title. But an equal part was the career timing for each. O'Neal had fought through ego wars in Orlando with Penny Hardaway and in Los Angeles with Bryant. Turning 33 that season, he didn't want his legacy to be one of a talented champion but troubled teammate. Enter Wade, who in his second season was willing to grant O'Neal his greatness while growing into his place in the league.

They understood this intersection of time, place and opportunity, too.

"Unfortunately, Shaq has been with two unbelievable players, Penny Hardaway when he was in

Legendary coach Pat Riley came out of retirement to coach his superstars to an NBA title.

Orlando and Kobe Bryant, that felt like they had more to give and they wanted to show more," Wade said that season. "But players are different. That's not my mind state. My mind state is getting the W first. And I know that with the wins and with the championships come everything you want."

O'Neal, the self-described "quot-atious one," connected the dots of Hardaway, Bryant and Wade in his own fashion.

"The difference between those three is in 'The Godfather' triology,' " O'Neal said. "One is Fredo, who was never ready for me to hand it over to him. One is Sonny, who will do whatever it takes to be the man. And one is Michael, who if you watch the trilogy, the Godfather hands it over to Michael. So I have no problem handing it over to Dwyane."

What O'Neal learned to his delight was that the book on Wade was an accurate one. He did put winning first. He did care about his teammates. While Bryant thought nothing of firing up 28 shots a game, Wade would cringe at taking anything more than 20 shots. And only then if he was making a high percentage of them, as well as contributing seven or eight assists, as many rebounds, and a couple of blocks.

"Plus a win," he said.

Occasionally, as events moved forward, O'Neal would double-check that Wade hadn't changed, Before their second season together in 2005-06, he asked Wade, "How many points do you want this year?"

Dwyane Wade

"What are you talking about?" Wade said.

"Your scoring average. What do you want it to be?" Shaq said.

"Aw, you know that doesn't matter to me," Wade said. "I just want to win."

At the end of their first year together, they expected to win, too. O'Neal struggled early in the playoffs with a deep thigh bruise, so Wade picked his game even higher. First, in sweeping New Jersey in the first round, he became the seventh player in a playoff series to average more than 25 points, eight assists and six rebounds while shooting 50 percent. The other six: Bob Cousy, Oscar Robertson, Wilt Chamberlain, Magic Johnson, Larry Bird and Michael Jordan.

He showed his flair of personality on the court, too. When he hit a 3-point shot to end the series, he turned to rapper Jay-Z, who was sitting courtside. "That's how you end it!" he shouted.

Then in sweeping Washington, Wade raised his game even higher. His averages in points, rebounds and shooting percentage increased while only his assists "slipped" from 8.8 to 8. In doing so, he became only one of five players to record at least 30 points, 15 assists and five rebounds in a game. The others: Robertson, Johnson, Jerry West and Walt Frazier.

The eight names he joined through the first two rounds are all Hall of Famers. Each was named to the NBA's 50 Greatest list of top players put out in 1996. So everyone saw his name was going up in lights.

During the Washington series, coach Eddie Jordan ticked off the names you had to set up defenses to stop: O'Neal, Dirk Nowitzski, Tim Duncan and Jason Kidd.

"Wade is getting to that point where you have to

have a game plan to stop him," Jordan said. "We're really at that point now when you look what we're trying to do. We had three defenses set up for Wade and two for O'Neal."

For better and worse, Wade's impact against Detroit in the Eastern Conference Finals became the final proof of his meteoric rise. Through four games, he was averaging 28 points, 6.8 assists and 6.1 rebounds. He made such an impression across the full playoff spring that a basketball debate began: Who should have been the No. 1 pick of the 2003 draft, Wade or LeBron James?

"LeBron," TNT analyst and former Chicago guard Steve Kerr said. "He'd be doing the same kind of things

Shaq elevated his play on both ends of the floor once the playoffs rolled around.

against Dwyane is if his team made the playoffs."

"Dwyane," Hall of Fame coach and ABC Radio analyst Jack Ramsay said. "Look at what he's accomplished. You can talk all you want about Shaq and his impact. But Dwyane has led them to the playoffs and is leading them through the playoffs, too."

Then in Game 5, on a simple move he had made hundreds of times through the lane, Wade felt a sharp pain in his ribs. It was pain like he had never felt before. A torn rib muscle, he was told. No matter what he did for the next couple of days, he found no comfort. Sitting down. Laying down. It didn't matter. He

coudln't even sleep comfortably.

Wade tried to loosen up the rib area Game 6, then tried to numb it completely with painkillers. Nothing worked. He sat out the game. He played Game 7, but his contribution was a spurt of will in the third quarter that moved the Heat within a few, distraught minutes of the Finals. His body wouldn't let him match the moment of those minutes, though. It was Detroit that advanced.

It took another seven weeks before he felt good enough to shoot a basketball.

It would take another year before his mind healed. ●

Flash Forward

In one magical season, Dwyane Wade becomes NBA champion, Finals MVP and bona fide superstar

There he stood, the star's star, now star struck. Head nodding. Eyes admiring. A small smile working across his mouth. Hall of Famer Julius Erving, still cool, always regal, but years from picking up a game and spinning it on his finger, was courtside watching the Miami Heat warm up before Game 4 of the NBA Finals. Watching a particular Heat player, actually.

"There he is," Erving said.

Erving had been in a conversation about grace on a basketball court and self-invented style in an athletic sense. He had possessed such traits in his playing career in the manner other people possess blond hair or brown eyes. Michael Jordan also did, he said. All the great winners have done it in some form, in every game, and Erving had wandered around an answer, never quite finding what he wanted to say, when he stopped and pointed across the court to Dwyane Wade.

"Dwyane guy has it," he said. "You see the manner he plays, the way he carries himself, it's just something you sense. It's something everyone senses, believe me, especially the guys he's playing against. There's no faking it. No need. He has it as much as anyone you'll find."

Erving pursed his lips and nodded. "If anyone didn't realize it before, everyone's realizing it now," he said.

This was not the cool, measured manner a sporting legend like Erving generally talks of a third-year player. But then Wade had that affect on people across the full spring of the NBA playoffs. By the end of this Finals series, Heat coach Pat Riley had compared him to Magic Johnson, then Jordan; Detroit guard Lindsay Hunter put him above LeBron James; Shaquille O'Neal likened him to Kobe Bryant in the fact that they're both "great scorers–Dwayne just does it the right way;" and TNT analyst Charles Barkley compared Wade to Jordan and, well, himself in only the way Sir Charles could: "Beautiful players, beautiful people."

But it was perhaps New Jersey coach Lawrence Frank who offered perhaps the most telling line when asked how Wade ushered the Nets into the offseason.

"Dwyane Wade," Frank said. "I don't want to ever hear that name again."

Heat coach Pat Riley started mentioning Wade in the same breath as Michael Jordan and Magic Johnson as Wade's game continued to blossom during the 2005 season.

Let's be clear then: The Wade that entered his third season in November was not the Wade that left it eight months later. Even as Wade entered the playoffs, he typically was painted as O'Neal's junior partner. His sidekick. A player of consequence, no doubt, but still someone outside the stratosphere of superstardom and one who benefited greatly from playing beside a force of nature like O'Neal.

Dwyane Wade

By the time Wade caught the final rebound of the NBA season and launched it into the Dallas sky, however, a different picture had emerged. That's because while the record shows it was the Heat that won, the mind's-eye memories from the Finals all involved Wade. There was Wade pouring in 12 points in the final minutes of Game 3 to overcome a 13-point deficit; Wade scoring 17 points in the final quarter of Game 5, the final two on pivotal free throws with 1.9 seconds left for the win; Wade scoring 36 points and grabbing 10 rebounds in the finale of Game 6 to cement the Finals' Most Valuable Player award.

It had been that way the previous three series leading into the Finals, too. So this didn't just become his team across these playoffs. It became his time as well. These Finals were a just the lasting testament of that. The championship story changed from one of shoring up the legacies of O'Neal and Riley to becoming the coming-out party for Wade. Just as O'Neal and Riley had pushed.

"You be the first," Riley had told Wade in front of his teammates before playing Detroit in the Eastern Conference Finals.

Wade knew what Riley meant. Be the first from his basketball generation to grab a ring. Win before James, the No. 1 pick and anointed league savior (plus Wade's good friend). Win before Carmelo Anthony, who had won a college title at Syracuse. Get a NBA ring before any of those players drafted ahead of him, considered better than him, or who like Yao Ming or Amare Stoudemire had been around longer than him.

A pro title, Riley knew, separates the players who can win from the player who is the winner.

Wade knew he was ready for this, too. His game, his confidence, his hunger, his place in the league—it was all in order by the time these playoffs rolled around. He had prepared himself, brick by brick, over the previous two seasons. He even had double-timed his workouts after the painful way the previous series against Detroit had ended. Once his injured rib healed, Wade enlisted Jordan's former strength coach,

Tim Grover, and began lifting weights to ensure his body wouldn't fail him again.

By simple measurement the change wasn't that much, just five pounds more on his body. But he felt stronger as he arrived in his third training camp that October. He came in such shape that he jokingly would flex in front of teammates to show off his biceps. "Pythons," he'd call them. Nor had he lost any of his body's explosiveness as his game showed each day.

Most importantly, he felt more confident in his ability to survive the NBA's grind.

"I'll keep trying to get stronger in different parts of

Wade has worked hard on his game off the floor through better dieting and a strict exercise regimen.

Wade celebrates a playoff victory against the New Jersey Nets at home with the fans.

my body so that I won't have the breakdown that I had," he said.

He hadn't undergone a total life makeover. He still had a 24-year-old's diet. Cheese steaks. Chips. Whatever he pleased. Sometimes, while adopting a stringent diet in mid-February to lose about 30 pounds, O'Neal's junk-food release would be to grab a handful of Wade's French fries. Wade's metabolism hadn't changed. Nor had his five percent body fat.

So everything Wade had worked on for two years, he then honed across another regular season full of change for the Heat. It was a roster that was torn apart by Riley for a consecutive off-season. The biggest trade in NBA history—five teams, 13 players—brought added talent but involved team-chemistry issues as well. Stan Van Gundy then resigned as coach in

December, and Riley returned to the sideline.

But for all the basketball change down the roster and Shakespearean drama at the top, the Heat's regular season eerily non-descript and strangely disappointing. O'Neal spent much of the time with his feet seemingly propped up on the desk, waiting for the playoffs. Others took his lead. Riley, upon taking over, said, "The team is a mess."

The Heat was 2-12 against division winners across the lackluster regular season. In February, after a nationally broadcasted drubbing in Dallas, TNT analyst Doug Collins noted, "This is not like a Pat Riley team tonight. Pat Riley teams don't quit."

Then there was Barkley, who was more direct during the network's studio show. "I blame the general manager–oh wait, he's their coach now," he said of Riley. "Gary Payton is their best point guard, and he's 77 years old. They don't have good outside shooting. They don't play good defense. They can't rebound."

So as November became April, as Riley became coach, as O'Neal became 34, as a Heat blueprint slowly and sometimes painfully dissolved into a different reality, it was Wade who provided the reminder of how good this team could be. Sometimes it was only him. He was the one the team turned to inn the clutch more and more.

It was Wade who scored the Heat's final 17 points in a February game against Detroit to rally it from a fourth-quarter deficit. It was Wade who waved off Riley's game-deciding play against Washington and called his own instead. "I wanted to open it up," he said. He made the crucial shot.

Wade turned a game against Cleveland into a one-on-one exhibition with LeBron James, each matching points and moments until Wade had finished with 44 points and nine assists to James' 47 points and nine assists.

"The bigger the moment, both of them stepped up even bigger," Riley said after that game. "I haven't seen players do that in a long, long time."

Still, the team paced itself through the long winter

Wade has emerged as a sturdy defender, as he demonstrates here against the New Jersey Nets' Jason Kidd.

while Riley grew infuriated and Wade quietly wondered whether all the bold roster moves would pay off. Even in the first round of the playoffs, the Heat not only continued its season-long sputter by dropping two games in Chicago to even the series, Wade and Payton also feuded in a public scene that became kindling wood for skeptics who had decided long ago that Riley's team would never jell.

The impetus for the fight was sluggish Heat play, and the spark was a Wade pass that bounced off Payton's foot. Wade shot a stony look at Payton. They argued in the timeout, Payton shouting, "Don't do that to me, I'm not your (expletive) boy."

Some teammates had to step in to separate them, and block out public eyes and ears. But Antoine Walker stepped in for a different reason, yelling at Payton himself. Like a boxing bell at the end of a round, the first-half buzzer sounded, and the Heat went to the locker room like something out of Noah's ark. Walker and Wade walked together, grumbling. Forty feet ahead, O'Neal put his oversized arm around Payton, leaned in and calmed him down.

"That's just something to fire up the team," said Payton, whose career has been marked by regular blow-ups with different teams. "It's sort of what Donovan McNabb and TO would do."

Never mind that McNabb and Terrell Owens helped sink the Philadelphia Eagles' title ambitions. Riley later would put a more positive spin on this episode after the series was won, saying his team underwent "trial by fire" for the emotional soul-searching involved.

Before that happened, another more worrisome crisis was coming for Wade. Just before half in Game 5, a particularly nasty fall left him with a bruised hip. He left for the locker room, where he took a painkiller—"a little shot in the butt," he said—and received treatment as precious seconds ticked away in the third quarter. Finally, with the Heat down by five points, with the series up for grabs midway through the quarter, O'Neal sent word after picking up his fourth foul:

"Get out here. We need you."

Wade returned, scored 30 points in the win and soon the Heat was cruising to the second round. This, however, would be a recurring, unwanted theme for Wade across the playoffs. Previously, in Game 2 against Chicago, he had to be helped to the locker room, limping badly. As the minutes went by, Heat fans wondered if this season would have the same,

star-crossed fate of the previous year against Detroit. It was just leg cramps, however. Wade returned to score 30 points.

Ahead, in the New Jersey series, a misplaced elbow would lay Wade out on the court in Game 2 and bloody his mouth. Once it was determined stitches weren't necessary, he continued merrily on his way to score 30 points that game, too. Other, more serious physical concerns were waiting against Detroit and Dallas, prompting teammates to joke Wade was having his life imitate his art. A Converse ad campaign had been released around the seismic falls Wade took to the court. "Fall seven times, get up eight," it said, mixing video clips of Wade's tumbles dating back to high school with the indomitable moral of the Japanese proverb.

Questions lingered about more than Wade's health after the opening game against New Jersey. The Nets threw an opening punch at the Heat, scoring 38 points in the first quarter en route to an easy win. Jason Kidd was the star, scoring 22 points with nine rebounds and seven assists.

"Every year people throw out a new guy like Dwyane Wade or Tony Parker," New Jersey forward Richard Jefferson said. "It's crazy. No one brings it like (Kidd)."

The night before Game 2, Wade and O'Neal met late at night to shoot free throws at American Airlines Arena. This had become a regular occurrence between the two. They met about 10 p.m. on the Heat practice floor. They shot. They talked. They joked. On this particular night, they decided the direction of the season was in their hands.

"We discussed what we needed to do," Wade said. "We knew how it was important for us to get the next game, to come out and play the way we knew we could as a team and we really hadn't yet in the playoffs."

Riley reveled in what he saw the next morning at the game-day practice. "You could almost sense in Dwyane that he was in a little different state."

He attacked hard that night. He owned the lane, as

usual. He also made three 3-point shots in the first quarter, tying his career high for a game. The Heat took a commanding 41-19 lead and was never threatened. If there was a game that started the Heat on its run through the next six weeks, it was this second one against the Nets that provided a glimpse of how well an uncertain roster could perform on its best nights.

Wade's game, too, was blossoming in that Nets game. For three years, the book on him was to allow him an outside shot. But with two weeks left in the regular season, back about the time the Heat locked into a playoff position, Wade knew he would play

Wade's World

Flash slashed and dashed his way through New Jersey and led the Heat in scoring and assists in the five-game series.

less to rest his body and began to work on the final part of his game.

It had been on his mind for a while, but it began one day after practice when he started what he always did, shooting from one spot near the top of the key and then running to another spot to shoot again. Back and forth. Shot after shot. Swish. Swish. Swish.

By now, Wade felt he had mastered the mid-range shot and the pull-up jumper. All the work on balance, on simple fundamentals, had paid off. So after this particular practice, on the verge of the playoffs, he experimented with the final step: The 3-point shot.

"Let's back up," he told Spoelstra.

Spoelstra worked with Wade on shooting each day after practice going back to his rookie year when they spent months on the foundation of body balance.

Spoelstra, this day, rebounded the ball and passed it to Wade beyond the 3-point line. Swish. Another shot. Swish. And some more. Swish. Swish. Swish.

"It felt the same as where I'd been shooting," Wade said.

This surprised and emboldened him. His philosophy was to add a weapon each off-season, something to take his gave up another notch, and he realistically expected to develop the 3-point shot over that summer. He had never developed much of a deep outside shot, making just 24 percent of 3-pointers in his three seasons. Nor was it a necessary part of his game.

In 75 regular season games this latest season, he took only 76 3-point shots. That was a career high, too. That would change in the playoffs. It spoke of his newfound confidence that he would make more 3-

Wade's World

Dwyane Wade

Wade was determined to rise to the challenge against the Detroit Pistons in the Eastern Conference Finals.

point shots (14) in the playoffs than across the full regular season (13). Even better, he shot a respectable 38 percent on them.

Wade prepares to sink the game-winning free throw in Game 5 of the NBA Finals against the Dallas Mavericks.

Wade didn't measure his changed shot simply by numbers, though. The look on some opponents' faces said more. Vince Carter's face, especially. In Game 2 against New Jersey, as Wade made those three 3-point shots in the first quarter, Carter showed nothing. He kept his reaction under wraps. But when Wade came out early in Game 3 and made another early 3-pointer, that confirmed he had a new weapon. Carter let his guard down.

"Vince looked at me, like, 'Uh-oh,'" Wade said. "I just smiled."

Wade shot six of nine on 3-pointers in the series. That made him, "unstoppable, man, unstoppable," as

Jefferson said at the series' end. In Game 3, Wade nearly had a triple double with 30 points, 10 rebounds and seven assists. Game 4 was almost an exact copy: 31 points, eight rebounds, seven assists.

It wasn't his just offense, either. With one second left in the clinching Game 5, Spoelstra told the Heat exactly what play the Nets would run out of a time-out. It was the assistant's job to break down opponents' out-of-bounds plays. The time remaining, the location of the inbounds pass and the one-point Heat lead narrowed the possible plays to the one he diagrammed during the time-out: Kidd would inbound the ball to a moving Carter.

Dwyane Wade

"I'll be ready," Wade said.

As Kidd threw the ball to Carter, just as the script read, Heat forward Udonis Haslem bumped Carter to throw him off. Wade then intercepted it to preserve the win and threw it high into the stands to start the celebration. The Heat had found its missing gear in winning four straight against the Nets. Likewise, it set up the rematch with Detroit in the Eastern Conference Finals that everyone wanted to see–including Wade.

The playoff loss to Detroit the spring earlier still weighed on him. O'Neal, too, had been so despondent afterward that his emotions surprised Riley and Van Gundy. Now, as they shot together in their late-night rendezvous, they talked about what this series meant to each and how ready they were.

Wade, perhaps, was too ready. He had three offensive fouls in the first half of the first game against Detroit and spent long minutes on the bench. The foul

trouble limited him to a playoff-low 27 minutes.

But when he was in the game he was on, making nine of 11 shots and seven of nine three throws for 25 points. What's more, Detroit's Tayshaun Prince and Chauncey Billups, both named to the NBA All-Defensive second team, could find no answer for Wade as the series unfolded.

In the next three games, Wade scored 32, 35 and 31 points at an exceptionally efficient rate. He was shooting 66 percent from the field. Not coincidentally, the Heat took a 3-1 lead.

"Toughest guy to cover in the league," Prince said of Wade.

But in a Game 5 loss, en route to scoring 23 points, trouble once again struck. During the game, Wade felt overheated, sticky, uncomfortable. The arena air felt smothering as the game went on. The problem soon surfaced. He awoke, sweaty and feverish, at 3 a.m. the

Wade splits the defense
of the 2004-2005
defending NBA
Champion San
Antonio Spurs.

Wade and the Heat battled the Los Angeles Lakers and Kobe Bryant during a highly anticipated matchup on Christmas Day, 2005.

Wade emerged as an indomitable force on the game's biggest stage as he led the Heat in scoring in every game of the NBA Finals against the Mavericks.

morning of Game 6. He began throwing up. At 8 a.m., he called team trainer Ron Culp, who sent him to the hospital for intravenous liquids.

"Not again," Wade remembered thinking to himself.

And so, before another Game 6 against Detroit, Wade looked in trouble and by extension the Heat did as well. He took the court that night sniffling and shiny with sweat. As if to confirm his discomfort, he made just one of six shots with three turnovers in the first quarter. He returned to the locker room to attach himself to an IV, receive more fluids and try and will himself to be healthy.

Nothing else resembled the Heat's history with Detroit. Jason Williams made his first 10 shots of the night to cover for the missing Wade. And when Wade did return late in the third quarter to a standing ovation, the Heat led by 12.

"I was ready to take over," he said.

He immediately supplied the finishing touches: A lean-in shot, then a jumper followed by two fadeaways and a highlight-reel double-pump turnaround. The Pistons were done. The Heat was moving on. And that evening after clinching, he turned to Alonzo Mourning and said, " 'Zo, can you believe we're going to the Finals?"

In many ways, Wade's slashing style arrived on basketball's biggest stage at the perfect time. The NBA's new rule changes outlawed a defender's merest touch on the perimeter. The hope was for a basketball renaissance that allowed free-flowing offensive beauty, highlighted superstars and generally recouped a game hijacked a generation earlier by the flexed-muscle brand of basketball of Riley's Knicks teams and the Bad Boy Pistons.

Wade became the new game's centerpiece.

"If you ever watch Dwyane attack, really attack, he is so low to the ground that once in a while it looks like he's really going to go to his knees," Riley said. "He has created his own signature game."

On a stage like the Finals, if the new rules didn't help pull back the curtain of Wade completely, Dallas helped as well. It made strategic oversights. First, Dallas players hadn't downloaded the latest bit of information about his outside shooting. Asked about defending Wade before the series, forward Josh Howard told reporters, "For the most part, shooting is one of his weakest areas." Guard Devin Harris said Wade wasn't different than Phoenix's Steve Nash in the previous series because, "He's not a good jump

shooter, not as good as Steve."

All this served as motivational fuel for Wade. "I've been hearing it as long as I've been playing this game," he said. "So it really doesn't matter to me. I'm going to play my game. You know, I don't worry about what my opponents say about me. If my jumper is there, it's there.

"If they are going to let me shoot, that's fine. I think I've proved I can make shots."

The other piece of Dallas thinking that benefited Wade was how coach Avery Johnson plotted his defense against the Heat. O'Neal got double- and sometimes triple-teams against him. He had trouble getting the ball and, when he did, had more trouble moving around the defense. This was a first these play-offs—O'Neal getting most of the attention while Wade was the responsibility of one defender. The fact that Dallas won the first two games only convinced Johnson it was the proper plan.

As events played out, there were other factors in play the first couple of games, too. Wade's illness from the Detroit series lingered. He couldn't shake it. After making six of seven shots in the opening quarter, his legs wilted under him. He felt like he was running uphill. He shot a timid five-of-18 the rest of the game.

"He had no energy," Spoelstra said.

Just how much Wade wanted this moment was obvious as the Heat went home down two games. He felt his health returning. He then considered the manner Dallas had played, especially studying the defense keying on O'Neal. He figured it was up to him to crack it and said as much to O'Neal during one of their late-night shootarounds.

"D-Wade told me if they were going to do that he was going to take over the series," O'Neal said.

He waited almost too until late into Game 3 to do so. And he did only then after picking up his fifth foul early in the final quarter, after Dallas went ahead 13 points with about six minutes left. The Heat had the look of a team left like litter on the road. Oh, and he had injured his knee in the game, too. A collision had

sent O'Neal's 330 pounds into Wade, and as the law of physics mandated it was Wade's knee that bent the wrong way. This would have been deemed calamitous misfortune, if it weren't for the way Wade took over the game at the end.

In these final minutes, he etched his name among NBA immortals like Magic, Bird and Jordan by scoring 12 points and single-handedly bringing the Heat back from the brink. It started with a bank shot off a drive. Then he made a driving 3-point play. He scored from the corner. Then drove for two more. Another jump shot.

Dwyane Wade

Wade would finish with a game-high 43 points to go with a game-high 13 rebounds. But his game-winning play came on an assist. Down a point, on its final possession, Wade knew what everyone else did: The Dallas defense would collapse on him. He saw Gary Payton standing open. Payton hadn't taken a shot all night. He took Wade's pass and drilled this one with 9.3 seconds left for the win.

In many ways, Riley would think later, this final play was the quintessential Wade. More than scoring. More than the ballet moves. More than the fame and glitter that had begun accompanying him, Wade remained about winning. This pass showed that. Other stars would trust only themselves at a moment like this. Wade trusted his team, too.

"He just rises to the occasion," Riley said of Wade. "He kept making play after play after play."

That ending convinced Dallas to change its defense. O'Neal wouldn't be its focus anymore. Wade would be. But after scoring 36 more points in the Heat's Game 4 win, Avery Johnson just became another coach in these playoffs left mumbling over how to defend him.

First there was Chicago coach Scott Skiles saying, "You can't let him split the defense, and he did that to us all series."

Then New Jersey's Frank admitting, "Keeping him from the rim is easier said than done."

"He's very good at finding the seams in the defense, so you've got to make sure the defense stays perfectly together," Detroit coach Flip Saunders observed after his team lost.

Now it was Avery Johnson's turn. After Game 4, he said: "Put it like this, when we've tried to contain him one on one, he's gotten around us. When we've tried to quick trap him, he split the quick traps. When we've tried to slow trap him, he's spun out of the slow traps."

Wade, to be sure, was driving to the basket with merciless intent. Dallas' front-line defenders often could only stop his lay-ins with fouls. Wade's 18 free-throws in Game 3 were only appetizers to the 25 and

21 in Games 5 and 6, respectively.

Game 5 turned on those free throws, too. Wade had begun the night awfully, making just three of his first 15 shots. From there he was nearly unstoppable. He ended with 43 points. He made a driving bank shot with 2.8 seconds left to force overtime. There, leaving the final time-out huddle, he re-thought Riley's set play.

"Coach, I want to go left," he said.

"Well, tell Shaquille to move out of there," Riley said.

Wade, in fact, drove twice to the right before reversing himself and pressing the accelerator by three Dallas defenders. One of them, Dirk Nowitzki, was whistled for a foul to give Wade his 24th and 25th foul

Dwyane Wade

Wade averaged a Jordan-esque 34.7 points, 7.8 rebounds and 3.8 assists per game in the Finals.

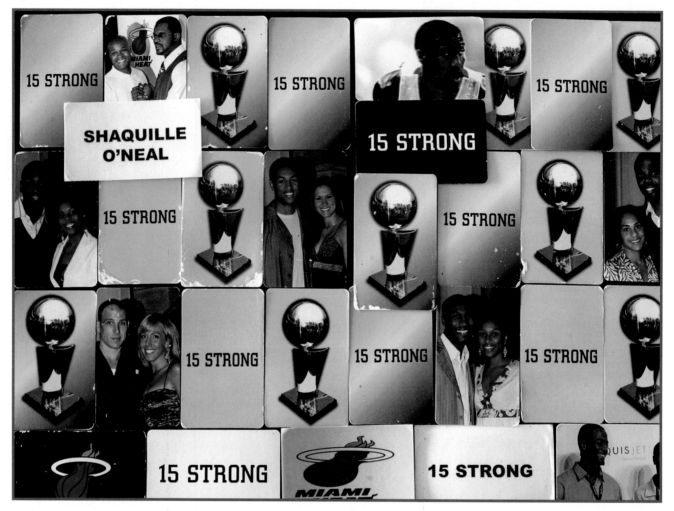

The Heat adopted the motto of "15 Strong" during their run to the title, which meant that all 15 players on the roster were an important part of the team.

shots—as many as the entire Dallas team. Down a point, he had to make both shots for the win. The previous night, as Wade practiced his foul shots, his cousin stood under the basket and said he would miss, that he wasn't any good, whatever, to try and mess with his focus.

That's what Wade thought as he stood at the foul line at the end of this overtime. "His face, right there underneath the basket, in my ear telling me I wasn't that good," Wade said.

He made both foul shots. The Heat won by one.

"As good a game as I've ever been around," Riley said.

And so it was back to Dallas for Game 6. The basketball world understood the torch that was being

passed now. O'Neal remained a presence, a big-body force no team could match. But at 34 he was less the Shaq of old and more an older Shaq. He would average just 13.7 points in the Finals to go with 10.2 rebounds. His playoffs-long scoring was better, but that 18.4 points a game still represented a career low.

With each passing game, the Finals was becoming Wade's show. Dallas owner Mark Cuban was even putting Wade at the center of a Jordan-esque double-standard of officiating. Cuban had stormed the court

and yelled at officials after Game 5, presumably about their call that gave Wade the final foul shots. He then glared into the stands at NBA commissioner David Stern. He also held a news conference after the game charging the officials missed a back-court violation on Wade in the waning seconds (the NBA corrected Cuban on his rules interpretation).

Returning to Dallas with the series still up for grabs, in other words, meant running into some Texas-sized emotions. Not only were the Mavericks a game away from losing, but they felt conspired against. Riley countered by bringing the tub of cards filled with a playoff-long motto of "15 Strong", relating to the 15 roster players.

But in many ways Riley knew that over-stated the case. As he even admitted after this final game, "Never have I leaned on two players more on a team."

O'Neal played another limited game, too. Nine points. Twelve rebounds. Clearly, the Heat's fate fell again to Wade. Predictably, too, he was unstoppable. He was as efficient as ever, making 10 of 18 shots and 16 of 21 free throws. That gave him 97 free throws for the Finals, a testament to his relentless attacking with the basketball.

Four of those foul shots by Wade finished off Dallas. For good measure, he grabbed the final rebound of the season and flung it into the Dallas night. Immediately, the celebration began, as well as Wade's comparisons to Jordan.

Wade downplayed them all, saying, "There's only one Michael." He did allow how Jordan, "was like a second father to me, because he was the guy I watched growing up and I felt like I was a part of. The comparisons are flattering, but I stay away from them. There won't be another Jordan."

Game after Finals game, the national media had asked Riley about it.

"Dwyane has told me that he would not like me to speak of him in context with Michael Jordan anymore out of respect of (Jordan)," he said. "He's a pretty good player himself. I think it's time for Dwyane to take on

his own persona."

In the winning locker room, as champagne sprayed, the winners hugged Wade, sometimes with tears in their eyes. There was Alonzo Mourning, having received doctor's permission to sip his first alcohol since a kidney transplant put his life in jeopardy and this career goal in doubt. There was Riley, who hadn't won since being with the Lakers 18 years earlier and said, "I would've traded all the others for this one."

O'Neal won in another city, with another star team-

Exhausted but satisfied,
Flash cradles his NBA Finals
MVP trophy.

mate, giving Los Angeles something to think about and adding depth to his legacy. Gary Payton got his first ring. So, too, did Heat owner Micky Arison.

But there was no doubt who the Finals' Most Valuable Player was, a fact underlined by Wade winning the award in a unanimous vote by the media. He finished with four consecutive games over 35 points to join Jordan, Rick Barry and Elgin Baylor as the only players to accomplish that in a Finals.

It wasn't just points, though. In the final game of a pressurized season in which the Heat had turned over its roster, switched coaches, picked up well-informed doubters and squabbled amongst themselves at time, Wade was the ultimate team player. He added 10 rebounds, five assists, four steals and three blocks in the finale.

And there he stood in a corner of the winning locker room, up on a bench, head near the ceiling, saying, "I'm a kid in a candy store. I'm living the dream."

Behind the cameras and reporters, his wife, Siohvaughn and agent Henry Thomas laughed. Thomas remembered his first meeting with Wade a few years earlier. Thomas, who also is from Chicago, had called through the proper channels to pitch his services. Looking back, however, he realized that Wade already had studied up on him through one of his clients, Tim Hardaway.

"Dwyane always had a plan," Thomas said. "You know how you meet some young people and they don't hear you or care what's being said? Dwyane focused on everything. And he really hasn't changed at his core. That's the remarkable part. He hasn't let any of this go to his head."

As if on cue, in humble 'Wadespeak', the newest Finals' MVP looked at the trophy in his hand and answered what it meant by saying, "This is a team award. Just like it's a team championship."

But from the men who rode on his back, who wore a ring for one reason above any other, the words came out differently.

"I just gave him the ball all playoffs and got out of

the way," Jason Williams said.

"He's the best right now," O'Neal said. "That's all you can say. He's the best."

"You all witnessed it," Riley said. "You all watched it. Players like that are hard to come by, and to watch them grow right in front of you. That's what these events do. They make genuine stars out of some players. He's making his legacy in his third year. We are blessed to have him." ●

Wade shows the NBA Finals MVP trophy
to Miami fans along a parade route
down Biscayne Boulevard.